The Lower East Side

The Lower East Side

A PORTRAIT IN TIME · BY DIANA CAVALLO

WITH PHOTOGRAPHS BY LEO STASHIN

CROWELL-COLLIER PRESS, NEW YORK

COLLIER-MACMILLAN LIMITED, LONDON

Library of Congress Catalog Card Number: 75-127459

The Macmillan Company
866 Third Avenue
New York, New York 10022

Collier-Macmillan Canada Ltd., Toronto, Ontario

Printed in the United States of America

10   9   8   7   6   5   4   3   2   1

*To Henry for the
pleasure of our many walks
through these old streets*

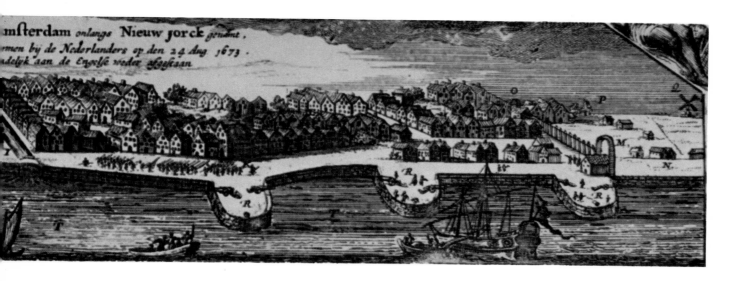

mſterdam *onlangs* Nieuw jorck *genant*.
men bij de Nederlanders op den 24 Aug 1673.
adelyk aan de Engelſe weder afgeſtaan

ACKNOWLEDGMENTS

The author would like to express special thanks to the people, the books, and the places that have been most helpful in putting together this volume.

The single most useful tool has been the over five hundred page collection and comment to be found in *The Columbia Historical Portrait of New York* by John Kouwenhoven. This book is a treasure-house of old prints and careful research, and nothing has been so important to the preparation of this book as that fine collection and study.

The staff and publications of the Museum of the City of New York and the South Street Seaport Museum have also been of great aid, and should be especially mentioned at this time.

The work of Ada Louise Huxtable, both in the *New York Times* and in her fine book, *Classic New York*, has provided a useful background and much interesting information.

I would also like to express my thanks to Michael Garber for his interest and enthusiasm, and for the benefit of his work in the Puerto Rican communities of New York.

PICTURE CREDITS

Brown Brothers, 71; Culver Pictures, 91, 112; George Eastman House (Lewis W. Hine Collection), 66, 83, 104; Library of Congress, 54, 58; Museum of the City of New York, 7, 9, 10, 25, 30–31, 35, 43, 73, 82 (above left and below), 116, 121; — Edward W. C. Arnold Collection, lent by the Metropolitan Museum of Art, 33, 82 (above right); — J. Clarence Davies Collection, copyright page, 29 (below), 36–37, 60–61, 81, 98, 101; — Jacob A. Riis Collection, 26; New York Historical Society, 46; New York Public Library (I. N. Phelps Stokes Collection), 12, 29 (above left), 92; South Street Seaport Museum, 20, 21, 40; Leo Stashin (from Rapho Guillumette), frontispiece, 2, 5, 6, 11, 15, 18, 22, 27, 29 (above right), 34, 39, 47, 49, 59, 64, 65, 70, 72, 76, 77, 78, 85, 88, 90, 95, 100, 103, 107, 108, 113, 114, 117, 118, 124, 127, 128–29, 130, 132.

Contents

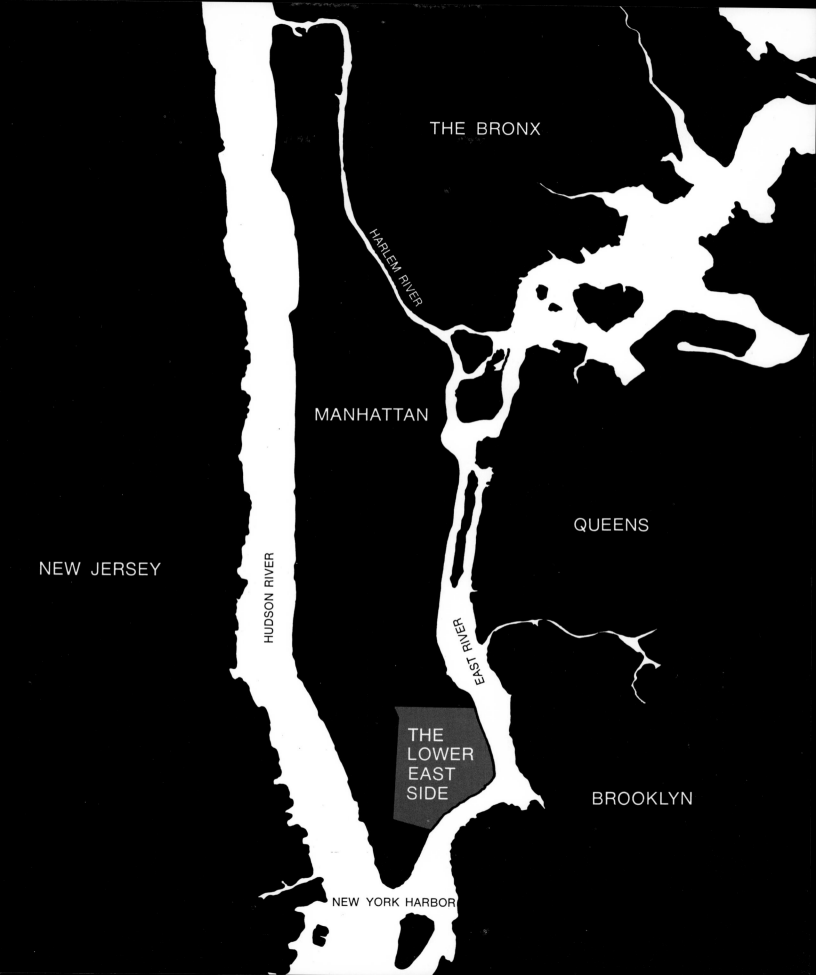

Towns

Within a Town

New York is very much a town. Or rather, it is towns within a town. It is Downtown, Midtown, and Uptown, and each one is divided and subdivided into still smaller towns and neighborhoods of its own. For even though New York is one of the largest cities in the world, holds more than nine million people, and spreads out in all directions from its island tip, it has never really lost its old beginnings. Only they are harder to find in the giant city and have become more valuable because they are so rare.

Neighborhoods or "towns" are hard for even the largest city to give up. Often their names and boundaries remain when there seems no longer any reason for them to be there. For who nowadays would expect a cherry orchard on Cherry Street, a wall on Wall Street, a canal on Canal Street, or a village in the Village? Yet these were landmarks that once meant just what they said, and they were very real once long ago. Often they have outlasted a thousand changes and will outlast perhaps a thousand more. Sometimes they have seen almost everything around them disappear until only *they* remain.

For *new* neighborhoods grow up around *old* boundaries that are already there. Or else new people move inside old "towns" and make them different. In this way, neighborhoods make less of a sprawling giant of a city. They break it down into its smaller and smaller parts. They make it still small enough to pry into and look around on foot. And only by seeing it close up can we peek into its hidden corners and search among its scrap heaps for forgotten treasures.

But knowing a city is not only fitting together broken bits and pieces of its past. It means finding how they came together to make *now*. It means seeing how even *now* is changing before our eyes. It means understanding that what is here today may be a different thing tomorrow. And it means that people

New York's past becomes harder to discover as the giant city grows and changes.

living in a future time will have even more bits and pieces to fit together. They will add *us* to all the rest—what we, in our time, will someday leave behind. Knowing a city means going *backward* and *forward* to get to right now.

Suppose something that happened in our neighborhood happened in yours.

A huge crane had just torn down a house. It left an empty spot where a whole house had been. Right next door, the neighboring house stood, just as always, in its place. But something we never saw before was there as well. The wall that once had joined them was open to our view now.

A strange outline seemed drawn upon the brick. It was the shape of an odd house, small enough to fit inside the one that had come down. With its sloped roof and chimney all its own, it looked more than anything like a farmhouse someone had traced upon the wall.

The crane that tore things down had left behind a "hidden house." All that time, without our knowing, this house had lived inside the other house and maybe inside many others in between. It had lived many years in hiding.

It was like a mystery in our own block. What was the shape on the brick wall? What did it tell us?

For one thing, it told us something else had been there—something far different from houses that we knew. Very likely it really was a farmhouse and our busy city street was once a farm. It may have been partly destroyed or burned, for there were wars and fires. Or else it was torn down to make room for newer, higher houses as the city grew and changed. The wall showed us how it once was. And when other walls went down, this outer one remained. It was used along with the

In destroying old buildings to make room for new, higher ones, we sometimes discover hidden stories of a city's past.

4

groundwork underneath, as part of the new house someone built in the old place.

We like to think we know our neighborhood better than anything outside our very own homes. After all, it is made up of places we pass every day—the houses of all our friends, the candy store, the schoolyard, the supermarket, the post office, the bank, the dry cleaner, the church. And yet, almost any neighborhood has hidden places that do not show unless we look—unless a crane or other cause of change exposes them to view. In this all city neighborhoods are alike.

Ours is the Lower East Side of old New York. It was there the crane tore down a house, showed us another sealed up inside, and set us thinking: What do we really know about the neighborhood we think we know so well?

It made us understand our neighborhood had many stories to tell—not stories in words, but stories in brick, in stone, in wooden beams, in broken pavements, stories around windows and in old cracks. The stories were in the neighborhood itself.

Grand Street today (opposite) and as a country lane in 1794 (above).

7

They had lived many years beneath the East River and in the parks and squares. They lived in the names of streets that never changed and some that did. They lived in houses, churches still there for us to see . . . in some that once were . . . and in those, too, that waited to be swept away like dust. Just like the hidden house, these tales were locked inside places, names, and streets —if we could only know them.

One day in 1906 workmen digging in lower Manhattan hit solid oak beams and timbers many feet underground. While working on a new subway they found the burned remains—the prow, keel, and frame timbers—of a ship three hundred years old. Some of its large wooden parts, "the *Tiger* timbers," are now in the Dutch Gallery of the Museum of the City of New York. They brought to sunlight a story of old New York before the early settlements sprang up.

It was called New Amsterdam in those days, and the *Tiger* had burned to the waterline as it was about to sail for Holland with its rich cargo of furs. The year was 1613, and the ship was so badly damaged it could no longer sail. Adriaen Block and his crew had the help of friendly Indians in cutting down trees along the shore and making a small new ship. Three hundred years later when the burned frame was found many feet underground, the shoreline was no longer at that place. Land had filled in a new waterfront, and now the buried remains of the ship were many feet from shore and had been covered over with hundreds of years of changes in the river, in the tides, and in the growing settlement, town, and city of New Amsterdam—later to be called New York.

When the *Tiger* burned, there were no houses for white men on Manhattan. Only the Indian lived there. Traders and

"The Tiger *timbers," preserved underground for three hundred years, tell an exciting story of old New York.*

8

explorers would come and go, living on ships, not even setting up small trading posts on land, depending on friendly Indians who came to them with furs in return for trinkets and who then disappeared once more into the forest. To build a new ship, Adriaen Block and his men had to spend many months on shore, living through the cold winter and working away through the spring. The Indians supplied them with much they would need and even helped them to build four bark huts—the first temporary settlement of white men on the island of Manhattan. Today the place where these four huts once stood is numbered 41–45 Broadway, and tall buildings rise almost from the water-line. They are places of trade and commerce very far from anything the hard-working Dutch sailors and Indians could dream as they felled the first great trees that lined the water at that site.

"The *Tiger* timbers" came from twenty feet underground to tell their story. They told it better than words and names, for

they stood themselves for what history books could only write about and say. They were themselves part of the busy ship getting ready to set sail, that burst suddenly into flame, with men running, jumping to save her, while great curls of smoke poured from her rigging and the air took on the smell of piles and piles of lost furs. But these burned timbers were not preserved three hundred years because anyone had thought to save them. Sometimes men are lucky that *time* helps them preserve the past when they have not saved it themselves.

But the crew of the *Tiger did* think of using some parts of the burned ship for the new one they would build. And so, the new ship, the *Onrust* (meaning "restless"), was fitted with some of the *Tiger*'s old parts. What happened to the old ship and the new shows us that the past can go on living in both these ways. It can be buried underground until someone finds

Today, Trinity Church (opposite) stands near the site where, in 1613, the Tiger's *crew built their bark huts, and used parts of their old ship to fit the new* Onrust (above).

10

it, or it can become part of a new thing, much like an old wall incorporated inside a new house.

The *Onrust* left behind it the cold winter of 1613 and the busy spring, the four bark huts and the small clearing on the shore. It went in search of new lands, and a larger, heavier Dutch ship to take its men and cargo home. The *Onrust* took Adriaen Block and his men up the East River, which they called Hellegat, or Hell Gate, into Long Island Sound, which they called "a beautiful inland sea." From there they went on to

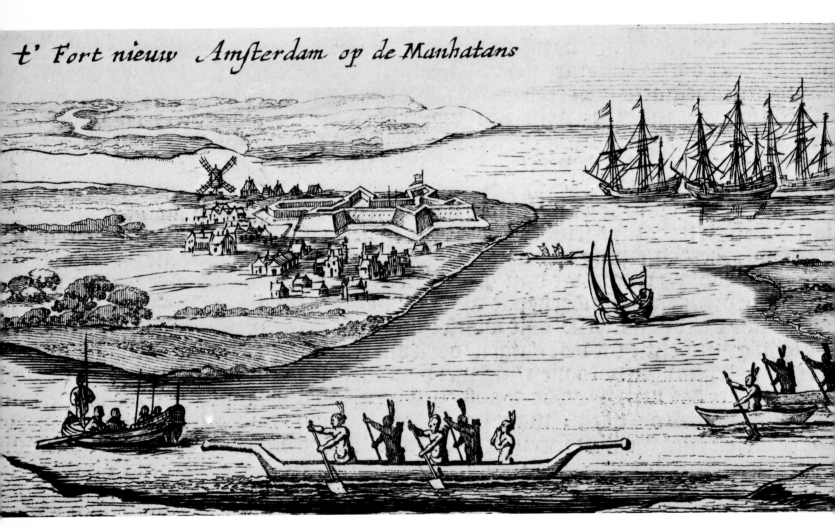

t' Fort nieuw Amsterdam op de Manhatans

find many of the inlets, capes, and bays of the rocky New England shore. The *Onrust* passed many lands and waters never before claimed or charted, not yet explored, and not even named. When at last they met a Dutch ship better suited than their own for the rough crossing back to Holland, they joined its crew. But some men stayed behind to lead the *Onrust* to still new rivers and new lands, to chart and name more future spots where one day new settlements would lie.

By the time Adriaen Block and his men returned to Holland, a trading fever had swept the country. His map of New Netherland, or "Nieu Nederlandt" as he called it, and his stories of the "Manhattes" tribe of Indians caused much interest. New trading companies were formed and more and more merchants were fitting ships to cross the seas. Before long, the four bark huts, lonely and empty along Manhattan's shore, became one of the busiest trading posts in the New World. And not many years later, in 1624, thirty families made the long, hard trip across the ocean—the first permanent settlers to make their homes in those very lands the *Onrust* had caught sight of the first time. It took them two months to cross, and once they had, they spread out through the lands that had been charted and named by Adriaen Block. Eight of the families settled the land along the East River; eighteen sailed up the Hudson; the others made their way to places along the Delaware and Connecticut rivers.

But the lower end of Manhattan Island is where the settlement of New Amsterdam began. In 1626 when another ship returned to Holland, it could report that the people lived there in peace, grew their own crops, traded many furs and skins, already had children born in the new land, and that, in the meantime, they had bought the island "Manhattes" from the Indians for sixty guilders—an amount that, whether accurately or not, is usually said to be twenty-four dollars in the present day.

Adriaen Block's map of New Netherland aroused great interest among Holland's merchants and traders. Shown here is the earliest known view of New York.

Nowadays the place where the city started is the busy heart of our Downtown. Uptown is now more famous because the city grew so far along the river—so far up and so far over—that it left its starting place farther and farther behind. But nothing is more interesting in a city than the place where its oldest and its newest things mix and mingle, and still live side by side.

Even what we call Downtown has spread out in all directions and grown huge. It jumped from a population of fewer than three hundred people in 1630 to one thousand by 1655. Over the years it has been filled *in* and filled *up* with thousands of buildings and millions of people. Today Downtown includes the Battery, the financial district, Greenwich Village, the East Village, and the whole Lower East Side. One of these parts alone, the Lower East Side, can be divided into still smaller neighborhoods of its own—Chinatown, Little Italy, and possibly others that someday will be well-known enough to go by a special name.

Only by looking more closely at one of the city's inner "towns"—one that is both large and small enough to be interesting and to explore—can we ever get to see New York from the inside. Looking in this way will be almost like walking around a neighborhood on foot, and going forward and backward in time into its smallest corners and narrow side streets.

No section of the city is better suited for this purpose than the Lower East Side, that immense cross section of the vast Downtown. For no neighborhood has kept more of its past alive and its present moving than this "town within a town" that stretches across Manhattan Island from just a little below Brooklyn Bridge to Fourteenth Street, and from the East River to Broadway.

14

The Lower East Side as seen from Brooklyn.

The River Town

Sometimes in the middle of the city, if you look up, you will see great flocks of seagulls circling in the sky. They swing around and around, flying in beautiful formation, diving and turning in the air. It may surprise you how often they are there, and how many there always seem to be. Then you may remember that water is all around you, that New York is surrounded by her rivers, and the skyscraper city itself, Manhattan, is an island facing out to the sea.

It seems strange that such a basic fact would be so easy to forget. Perhaps the city is so spread out that, unless you are almost on the water, it seems too far away to be there. Only if you take a boat around the island does it seem real, and only if you walk along the waterfront does it strike you how much the river means in the life of the city.

It is sad to many people that the river and sea are so soon forgotten, and that New York has let its waterfront get run-down and ugly. If you walk along the East River today—perhaps along the busy stretches on both sides of the Brooklyn Bridge—you will wonder not only why the city has done so little to keep its riverfront colorful, interesting, and clean, but why it has let it die. It remains busy, full of interesting points and places you must look hard for and dig out of hiding. But to do so you must step over fish heads and dirty puddles; you must walk around hundreds of trucks that not only use this busy riverfront but park there in the middle of the street; and you must bear the grime and smells of the modern warehouse and market.

This doesn't mean that yesterday's river and yesterday's markets were without their own ugly sides and dirty features. But the older things get and the more people there are to use them, the more care they need, and the more special help to stay well swept and well scrubbed—places to be proud of and

Seagulls remind us of a fact we often forget: that Manhattan is an island facing out to sea.

19

A model of the South Street Seaport Museum as it will look on completion by 1977 (left), and the "Street of Ships" as it appeared in 1855 (opposite). Schermerhorn Row can be seen in the backgrounds of both pictures.

to make people want to go there. South Street, which is one of the run-down streets along the river, was once called the "Street of Ships" and was one of the most popular places along the busy port—full of carts, wheelbarrows, horses, drays, merchants, errand boys, and especially the beautiful bowsprits of sailing ships pushed right up to the cobblestones of the street. It was a curious and exciting place to see. It was written about in books and visited by people. Important good things came from the changes in shipping and changes in trade—more goods, more jobs, more money. But with those changes the color and excitement of places like South Street were snuffed out. Up to now it has seemed that that old-time sailor's world was lost to the city forever.

Many cities want their waterfronts to be showplaces of the past and present, and New York—at last—has begun to understand that she must work to save hers. The walks along them must be made one of the pleasantest things that anyone in the city, on a bright sunny day, would ever want to do. And so, in a "tomorrow" not very far from now, this part of the "river town" near Brooklyn Bridge will look quite different from the drab and dreary waterfront of today. Some of the plans are being realized at this moment, and the complete waterfront renewal project should be completed no later than 1977. That is the present timetable, although many particulars may change in the process. But when that completion date arrives, real boats and real buildings will stand in the harbor area instead of the models and sketches that have had to serve the planners and public up to now on the drawing boards and in the files, museums, and libraries of the city. Along that finished "marina," as such waterfront sailing places are called, will stand the old sailing ships and paddle-wheelers from the 1800s that the South Street Seaport Museum has been seeking out and raising money to buy. Houses and buildings that were built from one to two hundred years ago and now are cracking,

peeling, crumbling as they stand, are to be saved from the wrecking crane and their present run-down condition and decay. A whole block, in fact, is to be carefully restored after long and special study, so that it will once again become the proud, handsome street the sailing city called Schermerhorn Row. An old market will be built in the same area, but a *special* market building that has been fashioned and drawn and finally built from old drawings and prints of another time—a market full of nooks and corners to peer into, curious shops in which to quietly stroll and browse, such things as sailmaker's shops, book stalls, and many other specialty shops not yet decided upon in the first plans. Still other ideas are being decided upon and may appear in the final marina strip when it is finished and in use. These include a restaurant high up in one of the buildings or on a rooftop facing the sea, modern apartment houses along the river or in streets nearby with a whole waterfront view, and a garden court, so that trees, plants, and flowers will add a touch of brightness and newness to the old scene. And, of course, there will be a much larger, fuller, and exciting seaport museum with more old models of ships, more prints and drawings, more sailor's gear and equipment. These all visitors may view after they have had a chance to look around and board the sailing vessels themselves and whatever other exciting specimens of ships will be moored in the harbor.

To do all this, the city and state have joined with the South Street Seaport Museum to make the waterfront section a landmark to be rescued and saved. This means not only helping with money but also passing laws to keep the land there from being sold for other purposes when the Fulton Fish Market building finally is torn down. The city and state are determined that whatever "new" takes over that special place will give an old charm, beauty, and excitement to the riverfront that it once had long ago. Many New Yorkers have joined the city and state in making this a "possible" dream by adding their names and

The famous Ambrose lightship is being refitted at the Seaport Pier as a museum of aids to navigation.

23

support to the membership of the Seaport Museum. Not long ago they raised money for their project by having a festival on the dock with a band and folk singers and guitars, but most spectacular of all was the sail they sponsored along the water-front itself. They rented an old side-wheeler for a cruise, and in ballgowns and tuxedos they dined and danced and looked back at the modern skyline of New York. Their eyes were on the seafront of *today*, but they saw *yesterday* and *tomorrow*, their fun and music helping to buy some of the nineteenth-century square-riggers, paddle-wheelers, schooners, and light-ships that one day will stand along the waterfront. In this way, the "Street of Ships" will not always be a name out of the past, but a name in the city's future as well.

Today if we walk along the East River from the southern tip of Manhattan, called the Battery, to Corlear's Hook, which is the turn the river takes before moving on up-town, and then beyond, we would trace the way the first settle-ment on Manhattan grew. Nowadays, taking that path, we would pass huge warehouses, large freighters and steamers in their docks, the Fulton Fish Market, the Brooklyn Bridge, the Franklin D. Roosevelt Drive, and East River Park with its bicycle path, river walk and benches, its tennis courts, football fields, basketball courts, and its amphitheater for concerts and plays. These were not thought of when wooden sailing ships went up and down the river with only a simple dock to load and unload goods, and all the land to Corlear's Hook and that little stretch beyond consisted of "bouweries" or small farms.

Some towns and cities grow according to a plan, while others just simply grow. New Amsterdam did both, following the course of the river as it went.

24

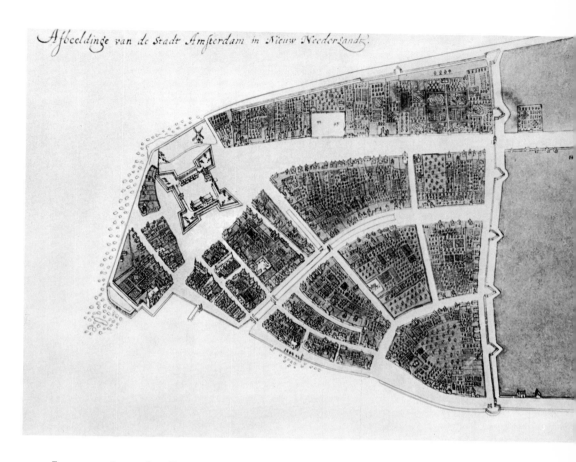

Afbeeldinge van de Stadt Amsterdam in Nieuw Neederlandt.

The original plan of 1660 for New Amsterdam shows the fort on the site of what is now Battery Park, and the wall (now Wall Street) that separated the town from the "country."

It started at the Battery, which is the closest natural entrance from the sea, so much so that when the famous writer, Herman Melville, speaks of it in *Moby Dick*, he says, "the Battery . . . washed by waves and cooled by breezes, which a few hours previous were out of sight of land." It got that name because a fort was there, close to the island tip, and a defense work of any kind was called a "battery" in that day. A fort was one of the first things new settlers always built in a strange land, and in New Amsterdam the fort was their protection near the sea.

The other thing they almost always built was a town wall, both as a boundary and for defense. This wall cut across the island from the East River to the Hudson, so the shape of old

25

The growth of New Amsterdam followed the course of the East River, just as the Franklin D. Roosevelt Drive does today (opposite). Long before the highway was built, the river was used for public bathing (above).

New Amsterdam was something like a wedge, with the fort as its tip and the wall as its long end. Everything outside the wall was called "the country," and so the town in 1640 or thereabouts measured no more than five hundred yards in its whole length.

We must remember that the island was smaller and narrower in that day. Sometimes we think only man-made things can change and the land itself, and rivers, lakes, and seas remain the same. Nothing could be further from the truth. The earth is always moving and with it all her tides, her bands of weather, her underground rocks and currents, and her glaciers. This natural change takes dozens, hundreds, even thousands of years to happen. Men often never see such change in all their lifetime. But they *can* see what they have altered for themselves in land and river beds, and this becomes amazing if we ever have the chance to live in one place long enough to watch it happen. And so, besides the natural change which was bound to make the shoreline different over three hundred years or more, there were also things the people of New Amsterdam and later of New York did to change the basic island size and shape.

Mud flats once lay along the rivers, and slowly they were filled in, built up, so that new streets were made along the Hudson and East River shores. Because of this, "the *Tiger* timbers" were found several streets inland instead of by the river where they would have been if the shoreline had not undergone such change. By building up the mud flats and making new streets, Battery Park came into being and in more recent times two superhighways were built along each shore: the West River Drive along the Hudson and the Franklin D. Roosevelt Drive on the East River side.

But it was a long time before superhighways and great bridges were to go along and cross the river. The plan for New Amsterdam called for a fort, a wall, and a dirt road to join them

The change from country to city is seen
in these three views of Union Square.

—one that was once an old Indian trail and that the settlers called Broadway. This was the whole length of town from one end to another—that distance mentioned before of only five hundred yards. Outside the Land Gate of the wall was "the country"—cow pastures, clover fields, valleys and streams, small farms and the larger one that went even as far as the present Fourteenth Street of our day, then a short ride "out of town."

The town itself grew and prospered between wall and fort and from river to river. Inside the fort, the settlers had built a church, a school, a governor's house, and a jail. And not far from this landmark stood another that was important to any Dutch town—a windmill to provide the settlement with power and to grind its wheat to flour. Another way the new town seemed like many others the colonists had left behind was the canal that went through one of its main streets—something they were very used to from their Dutch home.

It was mainly along the East River that the early settlers lived, all the way from the island tip to what was called the Water Gate of their town wall. Their houses stood in neat rows facing the river, with wharves, and docks, a weighing house, and warehouses all along the edge where they faced the sea. As the town grew, smaller docks were less important than a huge one that extended along the shore, and that was called, not surprisingly, the Great Dock. Travel across the river to Long Island became necessary as settlers moved to new homesteads, and trade between one point and another became brisk. A ferry was started to make trips back and forth, and its location was at Peck's Slip, near where the Fulton Fish Market now stands. This ferry landed at the present Fulton Street in Brooklyn and could be called by blowing a blast on a horn hung on a nearby tree, which resulted in the ferryman leaving his plow temporarily for a busy and profitable "second life" on the river.

30

The Peck's Slip ferry landing as it appeared in 1717.

This same Brooklyn Ferry was much changed by 1860. For one thing, it was much larger than the boat that went across the river from New Amsterdam to "Breukelen," as the other shore was called in its Dutch days. And for another, it carried not just one passenger or a handful at a time, but hundreds of persons, horses, and carts, in a way the farmer-ferryman of 1660 could not even dream. This ferry was the only way to cross back and forth between Brooklyn and Manhattan. This it did many times a day for the thousands on both sides who traveled to and from their jobs and went about their chores. This crossing was especially difficult, dangerous, and sometimes impossible in winter. For then the ferry had to push its way through ice jams and had to trust to terrible currents churned up by the wind.

If the ferry of the 1860s seemed an impossible dream to the old farmer-ferryman of 200 years before, this form of travel seemed already outmoded to another man who made this winter crossing sometime around 1868. It took several hours to go the otherwise short distance between Manhattan and Brooklyn, for in addition to everything else, the ferry was trying to plow through ice floes that blocked the river. As the other passengers shivered and shook, John Roebling, an engineer, began to plan a huge suspension bridge that could span the river, one that would be held up by two great towers rising like cathedrals from the shore. At the time no one believed a bridge could be built across the East River because it was far more than an ordinary river. It was like a shifting arm of the sea. But perhaps no dream endures like the one that people say can never be dreamed.

That "dream" which many men wanted and one man was challenged to carry out was the Brooklyn Bridge. It took four-

By 1860, the Brooklyn Ferry was carrying hundreds of passengers as well as livestock and cargo—an unimaginable dream to the early New Amsterdam farmers.

teen years to build, and it meant terrible hardship and back-breaking work by thousands of workmen before the bridge became the real and solid roadway we know so well. It cost the life of Roebling himself, although he thought any price was worth it. It claimed the lives of many others who, in those fourteen years, worked on the bridge and died in one way or another from the ordeal of sinking the high towers into the rock-bottom shore, or from stringing the cables, or in building the roadways across the bridge. It gave countless men the "bends" from too much pressure working underground. It crippled Roebling's son who carried on his father's plan and dream, forcing him to direct the rest of the work from a window in Brooklyn Heights, where he watched through binoculars as the second tower rose and the cables were strung.

33

The bridge was built only after the solid rock of the river bed had been blasted by gunpowder—a thing never done until that day. It was built even though a great fire broke out underground and everyone shouted as hoses sprayed, fearing that at any moment the tower might collapse. It was built although workmen refused to climb the cables and work over the charging river below until their courageous boss, a man named Farrington, proved there was less danger than they feared by riding the first cable strung across the river. Thousands came to the river's edge that day, and while excited men, women, and children of the city watched, Farrington moved inch by inch across the river on the sturdy steel cable that held him up— the crowds below seeming very small and very far away while they cheered, whistled, and sent up a happy roar.

When the bridge was finished in 1883, the day came when the president of the United States cut its bright ribbon and the first traffic could cross. Streamers were flying . . . boats blasted their horns . . . people were waving and shouting . . . and fireworks exploded high over the water to make beautiful

Farrington riding the first Brooklyn Bridge cable across the East River (above) and the bridge as it appears today (opposite).

35

flares and graceful designs. There has never been a more colorful or exciting celebration in New York. Perhaps so much pain and hardship had gone into the fourteen-year-old dream that more than any other public event of its kind it deserved the gay and spectacular opening that New Yorkers, the nation, and the world proudly gave it.

The Brooklyn Bridge is still considered today one of the most graceful and beautiful bridges in the world. Its webbing is more delicate than that of other bridges and the arc it makes as it spans the river is not leaden and tired as it is in many others. It would have excited the imagination of one of our finest poets, Walt Whitman. For he, standing where the bridge stands but speaking of the Brooklyn Ferry which he then thought might last forever, gave the best description of the land, the river, and the feeling which the two inspire from that place. He said, looking out over a hundred years ago at the River Town:

> *Others will enter the gates of the ferry and*
>   *cross from shore to shore,*
> *Others will watch the run of the flood-tide,*
> *Others will see the shipping of Manhattan north*
>   *and west, and the heights of Brooklyn*
>   *to the south and east,*
> *Others will see the islands large and small;*
> *Fifty years hence, others will see them as they*
>   *cross, the sun half an hour high,*
> *A hundred years hence, or ever so many hundred*
>   *years hence, others will see them,*
> *Will enjoy the sunset, the pouring-in of the*
>   *flood-tide, the falling back to the sea of*
>   *the ebb-tide.*

Although these are a poet's words on "Crossing Brooklyn Ferry," perhaps they best describe what rose in John Roebling's heart when he dreamed his magnificent bridge.

"The city of the Manhattoes," says the writer of *Moby Dick*, is "belted 'round by wharves as Indian isles by coral reefs —commerce surrounds it with her surf." It is no wonder that New York has grown along its rivers and that its life from early New Amsterdam to now has been largely decided by its trade. A trading company had founded it, and a trading town it remained. Even today it retains its trust and need of the sea and the flavor and smell of ships.

From the first, the settlers had depended on the busy coming and going of cargo between Holland and their little town. For only in this way were they provided with special things they could neither grow nor make themselves, and all the signs of riches—gold and silver candlesticks and cups, delicate glass and dishes—had to come from across the seas. All they had or were able to buy, except for what they grew and raised to feed and clothe themselves, was possible only through the Dutch West India Company. They prospered or failed in keeping with what they were able to provide, especially in valuable furs and skins, for the return trip of the company ship back to Holland.

England also kept a watchful eye on all that came in and went out of the busy port it had renamed New York. The city's wharves and docks were kept busy shipping to England much of the raw material she would need to fight her wars and produce her goods. The colonists were then forced to buy back the finished products that had been made with what they had sent over in a raw state, for these—such things as wool and cotton goods—they were not permitted to buy or sell except from England.

The countries of Europe were restless, fighting for power among themselves, and most of all, fighting for raw materials and new markets for their goods, which alone would make them first among nations. And this was done, when not by war, through trade. Their needs and the needs of the United States of America when it too joined the list of nations, threw New York into an ever increasing fever of commercial activity and trade.

The only way to keep up with all the goods to be shipped in and out of the port was to have more and more counting houses to handle the paperwork for merchants, marking down all that came in and went out, figuring up the charges, and arranging for transportation to places all through the city and up and down the coast. And the only way to keep up with the goods that had to move in all directions, and to keep up with the call of England and other nations for more ships, ships, ships, was to build new shipyards up and down the river. Soon the sloping farmland of the largest "bouwerie" of that day—the farm of Peter Stuyvesant, who had been director general of New Amsterdam from 1647 until the English sent their flag up from the fort in 1664—became the site of the great dock and shipyards of the New World. That same stretch around Fourth and Fifth streets on the East River where one of the many trails from "town" once led to deepest "country" provided trees to build and outfit the handsome clipper ships, barks, schooners, brigs, sloops, freighters, and packet ships, that were launched from the great yards.

Today shipbuilding has largely disappeared from the East River. Yet only 150 years ago shipyards overflowed the turn of the island at Corlear's Hook and even spread to the other side of the river. For part of the price of becoming a new and important power was that, from 1800 on, the United States

Shipbuilding near Corlear's Hook—a detail from the 1717 William Burgis drawing (see pages 30–31).

42

43

built ships not only for nations like Greece, Turkey, Russia, and France, but had to build a navy as well of her own. Across the river from Corlear's Hook the Brooklyn Navy Yard took on this job. For years the Lower East Side looked out across the river at warships being built, outfitted, painted, and repaired on the opposite shore. And although the old-time frigates became destroyers as time passed, and the old wood frames and sails were replaced by steel and steam engines, the Brooklyn Navy Yard continued supplying the United States Navy with ships until 1966, when finally the shipyards were closed down. For two years after that, no one was sure what the United States Government would do with the old Yard. In 1968 it was sold to the City of New York for $25,000,000, and in the same year the office of the mayor announced the city's plans for development of the area.

On the place where warships had for so many years been made and launched, huge buildings and plants will soon be added to the generators already there. These plants will burn and treat the tons and gallons of city garbage and waste. For just as the population of New York has grown so vast that it is almost impossible to house, clothe, and feed its people, so the garbage and sewer waste of the city has expanded so that there is no safe place for it to be. While there have been many disagreements on how and where this should be done, and many have fought to have these plants placed anywhere but right along the river across from the beautiful new marina project that so recently has been won, on two things almost all parties could agree: New York sorely needs such new services before the present ones break down, and to get them will cost one *billion* dollars.

As plans and sketches for this new project are carried out, some of the first ideas may change and give way to others that only later will seem better. It will take many years before the project is completed. The present plans call for garbage barges that will unload at a special pier on the river, and there will be five thousand tons of garbage hauled there and burned in its great incinerator every day. The sewage of the city will be treated there as well, although little is said of how this will be done. But it is expected that there will be fifty million gallons of it every day. The methane gas given off by the treatment plant will fire the burners. The special plant for burning—the giant incinerator—will give off so much heat that it will turn to power. This power can then be sold to generating plants nearby, and the money raised in this way can help to pay all the costs of getting our waste and garbage out of our houses, streets, rivers, and air.

These new power plants, when they are completed, will raise huge heads into the New York sky. Hundreds of years before, the grand arms of windmills provided a different power —water power—for the many uses of the town. Windmills turned in the New Amsterdam breeze and raised their arms across the river on the "Breukelen" side. They provided all the power the townsmen of that day could use and need. Yet they were handsome and picturesque to the eye as they dotted the East River shore.

How these *new* power plants of the city will look is the subject of much discussion in the present day. What the Lower East Side will see across the river from Corlear's Hook is only known in sketches and raises many arguments and hopes just now. These hopes are that when the necessary plants are built, they will be neither ugly to the sight, unpleasant to the smell, nor dangerous to the air we breathe. For a long time has passed since the pure country air, clear rivers, and fresh green of the first New Amsterdam days. Today, all fast-growing cities fight battles against dirty air and smog, unsafe rivers, and the crowded dingy look too many of them already have. Just as the

*The Brooklyn Navy Yard in
1855 (above) and today
(opposite). Huge power plants
will one day rise on the site.*

South Street Seaport Museum and the city and state have joined to save the riverfront, many interested people and officials of government are working to save the growing city from itself.

Though shipbuilding is largely a thing of the past, the East River has not been deserted by boats and commerce. But for the most part it has lost the passenger trade to the Hudson River. For not only are the clipper ships, packet boats, and old-fashioned steamers gone from the East River shores, but so are the great ocean liners, famous ships like the *France* and the *Michelangelo*. Millions of Americans who leave each year for business and pleasure trips to Europe, Asia, North and South America, embark at the piers that dot the West Side. This was not always the case.

In the old days when winters in New York were more severe, the East River was less likely than the Hudson to be frozen solid and so was more dependable and more often used. Packet ships, very popular for passenger travel, left from the South Street docks that made the East River waterfront the "Street of Ships." Nowadays only a handful of passengers choose to leave from these docks, sometimes joining the crew and cargo of freighters for a long ocean voyage with many cargo stops. For these are among the few large ships that have not moved to the more active Hudson River side.

Instead, the East River is now put to use by smaller or mostly hauling craft. It is a river of freighters, barges, tugboats, and the tourist lines that circle the island. The freighters are what keep the river busy and they sometimes turn out to be unusually handsome ships. Many, like the Belgian Line freighters, which used to dock for many years at Corlear's Hook, have their

own home dock, and are located where the old shipyards once were. Now high-rise apartment buildings line the river there, and many who live in them along Water, Montgomery, or on that same Cherry Street from the old "bouwerie" days, remember looking out their windows to see a familiar yellow and white freighter sitting almost in their own front yard. They would notice when, after long days among them, it would suddenly disappear for its other life of the sea. Only when it returned with bright flags waving did the neighborhood seem the same. For they had come to think of it affectionately for many years as their very own boat.

Besides these freighters there are the barges that go up and down the river strapped with heavy goods and supplies needed for the busy life of the present day. They are often loaded with railroad cars, wood, and coal, and they keep the river traffic brisk. The tugs, on the other hand, are among the most picturesque boats making the river trip. Sometimes they are painted bright colors that help make them stand out from the dull shapes of other river boats, and in addition they are topped by quaint smokestacks and go by strange, gay names. They seem to enjoy their role as guides to much larger, heavier boats that require their help to get through the difficult river channel.

Liners crowded with tourists circle Manhattan island and pass the East River shore several times each day. People line the railings to get a look at the famous skyline of New York, the Statue of Liberty, the crowded mass of houses side by side, the high-rise buildings, the bridges and roadways, the small islands in the river channel as they pass. For three hours they watch, snap pictures, chat, walk the decks, and often make a small picnic of the trip, bringing along their own lunches or buying snacks aboard the ship.

This liner gives us a good view of the "River Town." It rounds the Battery, where there is no longer a fort as in the old days. It passes the downtown skyscrapers that line Wall Street and Broadway and where once tiny Dutch houses stood side by side in neat little rows. It slips beneath the strong yet delicate steel and webbing of the Brooklyn Bridge. It pushes along towards Corlear's Hook, moving around it—that whole stretch where so many shipyards were.

Soon Downtown is almost left behind. The liner will follow along the East River Drive, plunge along the shoreline with it in pursuit of the great Uptown. Ahead, the uptown skyscrapers —the most beautiful and handsome in the world—are rising, and more frequent but less impressive bridges. In between is the Lower East Side—that land mass pushing out from the river around Brooklyn Bridge, rounding Corlear's Hook to reach Fourteenth Street where East River Park comes to a sudden end. In this crowded land mass old and new press close together—eighteenth-century houses, churches, spires, old tenements, new apartment houses, office buildings, rooftops of schools and stores, and chimneys smoking. Every space seems filled. Everywhere brick, stone, concrete, steel, and glass towers fill the sky. They are all there at once, beside each other—all that space filled *in*, filled *up*. There seems no place left for anyone to build. Yet surely there will be more people and more building.

Perhaps one day among those "more," another boy or girl will stand looking from the same river towards the same shore. Just as *we* find it unreal and quaint to think of the little Dutch houses set all in a row, the barnhouses and windmills, the farmhouses and hills, the forests, valleys, and streams, *they* may very well find thought of *us* strange and picturesque—all those brick, concrete, steel, and glass towers lined up like a fortress on the shore. Will some of those houses, buildings, towers be there to stand for us three hundred years from now? Or will they completely vanish so that the fact we lived at all will seem mostly like a dream?

The Market Town

54

Whenever settlers—or immigrants as they were later called—came from their old homeland to the new, they brought with them not only the goods they carried but things no one could *see*. For no matter where they came from or why they left, part of their hidden baggage included ways of doing things—ways they had always done them and which they never thought of giving up. Soon after they arrived, they would set about putting these old ways to work in the New World.

One of these "ways" was always Market Day. Almost all immigrants were used to having a special day of the week set aside for farmers, merchants, housewives, townsmen, and children to gather in the public square to display, buy, sell, and trade their wares. This was true in Holland and it was true in the New Amsterdam of the old Dutch days. It was true in the English towns and it was true in the New York of colonial times. It was true in the early days of American independence and in the later ones of the expanding nation. And it was true in each and every one of the great waves of immigration that flooded the country from 1880 to 1920. For from all the different parts of Europe and from Asia, the people who came and crowded into the many little "towns" of New York brought with them the ways of their old markets, and this meant also the special market goods they had grown used to and would miss so far from "home."

But Market Day was more than just a custom, more than a shopping center, and more than a tie to the Old World. It was the only way goods in the old town could move, change hands for money, and not rot or pile up in fields, in homes and on the many docks. It was a way people could make a living. In later years it meant "jobs"—a place on a street corner—to millions of people who came to this country with little more than what

Immigrants brought their market traditions as well as their possessions to New York. This Atlantic liner arrived in 1906.

they wore upon their backs. On Market Day that "place on a street corner" meant ready customers who would look over any goods a vendor would put together, and they had come to *buy*.

On Market Day more than any other, the vendor would set up early in the morning. Often he would simply hang all his wares upon his back, sling them across his arms and shoulders, and walk up and down looking for customers. Others, luckier than they, had the help of friends and relatives already here who got them started, perhaps with a pushcart or in renting a counter or stall. One by one new peddlers were added to the traffic jam of desperate people who had no other way to make a living and who sold their wares on the city streets. Often when they found other jobs as tailors or construction workers who were so much in demand, their places would be taken by three or four more newcomers who crowded into a single empty space. Others who had made money and saved it went on to open small stores nearby where Market Day customers could still seek them out as they had in the old pushcart days.

But before pushcarts lined the streets or special buildings were set up to house them, things were even simpler than that. The earliest market came into being in the settlement days when farmers and hunters would cross the river from Long Island and spread their wares along the ground. These "markets" were right where they unloaded, and there they would wait for other settlers to come by to sell their goods. Often this would depend on luck, and it became difficult to continue without setting aside a special day when people would know *where* and *when* they might find them. For just as these farmers and hunters needed to *sell* their goods, so the townspeople wanted to *buy*. Saturday was made the official Market Day, and from that first market place along the shore—the Strand as it was called— the market soon moved further back to the side of the fort. This became known as the Market Field. It was not very far from the weigh-house or custom house that had been set up along the dock. This weigh-house or custom house was important because all the goods that either entered or left the town had to be inspected there. All this was near the Battery end of the East River shore, even as our present Customs Building is today.

But in order to picture those early markets, you must imagine stall after stall of fruits and vegetables, butter and eggs, rows of preserved goods, jellies and jams, bolts of cloth and piles of linen. You must see the women looking for choice goods or making needed house money selling them, and chatting with neighbors and friends that otherwise they rarely had time to see. You must picture the men looking over farm animals that were up for sale and picking out pelts and skins they needed in their work and homes. While the women gossiped and shopped, the men would go off in small groups to nearby taverns to drink beer and take a few puffs on their pipes. You must imagine the children, too, for they were everywhere about —the older ones helping with farm animals and selling the butter and eggs, and the younger ones looking for toys to play with and finding new games among the counters or off a little way on the grass. You must see even the Indians, in peaceful times, joining in this old "way," sitting among the townspeople, smoking their pipes, their furs and game spread out before them, their handmade leather goods and strings of beads, all up for a good bargain or trade, and part of the public sale.

This kind of marketplace and a real Market Day have slowly faded from our modern lives. Only places like the Lower East Side of New York keep up the old market "way." There, where the ties to the Old World are still strong and fresh, you will find neighborhood markets that look, feel, and smell quite different from the supermarket world of the present day. Strange herbs are found there and unusual cuts of meat, types of fish not common to the American diet, great hanging cheeses, sausages, and special spices, nuts, and greens. They seem to be

Market Day on old Hester Street (opposite) and on present-day Orchard Street (right). The Lower East Side is one of the few places that maintains the market traditions of the immigrants.

The Fulton Street Market in 1834.

what you might find in the public square of some far away small town where strange languages are spoken. Those who have set up such markets in the New World and those who use them have remembered. They have carried these old ways across the seas as hidden baggage in their minds.

Buildings were set up to move the markets indoors. It is easy to understand why. A summer shower would send vendors flying to save their wares and customers running for cover. Whole days in April were lost to selling because of the steady rain. Winters were particularly harsh. Stalls could not open; customers would not come. Often the poor vendors nearly froze, or else had to keep huge bonfires blazing to keep warm, or they spent a good part of the day rubbing their hands over hot coals—if they could afford them. No wonder most of them barely made a living. And when they were forced off the street and into market buildings, many could no longer continue and left the streets to find work wherever they could.

But market buildings were set up mainly to protect the public. Often the city insisted that something be done about the terrible market conditions, which, though never of the best, grew steadily worse as more and more people pressed into the city. For one thing, the streets became so overcrowded with pushcarts they were often three and four deep on the sidewalk and spilled over into the gutter. And for another, they were seldom kept clean. The dust and dirt of the street did not help, and when asphalt was laid in the market streets, peddlers often fought against these new measures to the end. Soon after the shiny black streets were laid, they were again full of trash, puddles, and holes to the complete despair of city officials. Health inspectors were especially unhappy about the markets, for, except for issuing a license for each pushcart, there was little control the city could then have over them outdoors. In addition to the trash and garbage problem, the smells that were given off by the outdoor markets were unbearable to those who passed and impossible for those who lived there. In fact, the people who lived near the markets usually had among the worst living conditions in the city. Besides the heavy odor of fish and the stale smells of the market of that day, the noise and confusion crept into every room. The market people were up and about long before daybreak, and on the heavy Market Days they often stayed up and busy well into the night. Carts rumbled down streets; vendors cried out their wares; shouts of bargaining and argument filled the market air. These were not neighborhoods made for light sleepers or delicate stomachs. But worst of all, a place had to be found for that great mass of people who worked and shopped there. For they lived in these neighborhoods, crowding into their small rooms and tripling the number of people who should be in each apartment and in each house. But many of these markets and their problems came at a later time, after other markets had already marked the growth of the city and opened the way to that more widespread market life.

Years and years after the days of the Strand and the Market Field of New Amsterdam, there were two chief markets in the city. Both of these have continued to the present day, although they have either moved or are in the process of moving to other parts of the city. They have also become *wholesale* markets since those first days, which means they no longer sell to the customer who shops for a single family, but instead trucks are lined up outside their doors from the supermarkets, groceries, hotels, and restaurants of the city. It is they that buy there and then resell the products to you and to me in our own neighborhoods. The city has grown too big for it to be otherwise, and the markets only reflect what has happened to every other part of life in a huge metropolis like New York. There are markets for the markets.

The two largest wholesale markets in the country were set up in the 1800s and still exist today—even though they are no longer the same as they were then. In those old days the markets were on opposite sides of Fulton Street—the Fulton Market on the East River side between South and Water streets, and the Washington Market on the Hudson River side at Vesey Street. Today the Washington Market sells only produce—fruits and vegetables—and has already moved to its new home in the Bronx. This was done to reduce the jam-up of truck traffic in the downtown area. It was felt that the new expressways and superhighways that reach out to the farthest parts of the city are better able to carry the crushing burden of moving the city's goods and feeding its people. And it is the same expressways and superhighways that have carried the old markets far from their old beginnings near the old New Amsterdam town wall.

In its first days, in 1821 when it was built, and for many years thereafter, the Fulton Market sold almost every kind of food you could imagine. Today only fish is sold there and its name was changed long ago to the Fulton *Fish* Market. But once you could buy not only fish there, but meat, fruit, and vegetables. Because of its location on Fulton Street—right between South and Front streets on the East River—those who shopped there had a wonderful view of masts and sails in the background, flocks of seagulls circling the pails and nets. Inside, stalls were loaded with every possible kind of life found in the sea, with great sides of lamb, beef, and pork, hung on giant hooks, game birds, rabbits, and even live fowl crowding

the racks and being hawked in the market din. Fruits and vegetables were there in great abundance, overflowing counters. As the city grew, the markets had to give up doing so much of everything, and at that point the Washington Market took over the produce trade and the Fulton Market became the Fulton Fish Market.

It was the fish merchants who had always been more numerous than all the others in that place, and the Fulton Market became their special home. Only the same building did not house them forever. The old market building of 1821 was replaced by the new one of 1882. But even that one will soon be ground to dust. Over its ashes a new market will rise—a copy of a much older one that will go back to even earlier market days. It will not go back to Dutch beginnings, for Dutch houses and buildings were lost to our Downtown in the Great Fire of 1835. Some old buildings remain, though, from the days of the English rule and of the United States as it was before the

Today's Fulton Fish Market replaced the old Fulton Market in 1882, and will itself make way for a restored market as part of the South Street Seaport Museum.

time of the Civil War, around 1860. When the riverfront is restored under the plans set up through the South Street Seaport Museum, the Fulton Market will have already disappeared into its faraway home in Hunts Point, the Bronx. And a new market building will then be free to rise once more in the old Fulton Street place among the houses and buildings that will be rescued and restored, rebuilt to look like a world closer to 1800 than our own. The new market will be built from the oldest prints and drawings that can be found in our present-day libraries and museums. In a way, the market itself will be much like a library or museum, where people can browse around and mix for themselves some portions of the present and the past.

*M*ost Americans are from immigrant families. Some immigrants are simply more recent than others, or have been here for a longer time. Usually the longer people stay here the less they keep up the old ways and the less there are ties to old foods and customs. This is because after a while children and grandchildren who have never been in "the old country" do not find these ways as real and important as their parents and grandparents do.

The oldest Americans, the Indians, have preserved some of their old foods and ways, both because often they have lived apart on reservations and so have continued them, or else because their customs were quietly taken up by the new people who came. Nothing seems more "American" than the maize, turkey, and pumpkin of the earliest colonial days. Yet they were strange to the people who first came to this country from Europe. They themselves brought with them many foods and customs that joined with the Indian ones to make an "American" way of life and an "American" kind of cooking.

This Italian immigrant family seeking lost baggage was photographed by Lewis W. Hine in 1905. (George Eastman House Collection)

67

Like the Indians, the Blacks in this country do not have "old country" markets. Often they have been here for two hundred years or more, and so African foods and African ways have less meaning for those who live here today, for they are not only *years* but *centuries* removed from those old roots. It is also true that since they did not come of their own free will but were forced to live, work, and adopt the customs and ways of the new country, their ties with Africa were broken. Even though *individuals* were "indentured" or robbed of their freedom and forced to serve without pay, this did not happen to any other "immigrant" people as a *group*. If anything, the market and eating customs of Blacks have most in common with the South of this country because usually their most recent roots lie there. Most Southern cooking and market habits have been part of the country's past so long they are thought of as part of the "American" way.

For that "American" way is only partly what new and different people learn and take of the customs they find already here. The other part is what each new group adds always to enlarge and enrich that "way." What they add, instead of always remaining odd and different, becomes widespread and commonplace when enough time has passed and the new customs are more generally known. This means that yesterday's "strangeness" turns into tomorrow's "fashion" before you know it has happened.

The markets that have reflected most of all the effects of new immigrants upon the city were those that came into being around 1880, 1890, and up to 1910. These were the years of the greatest rush of people from all parts of Europe and Asia into the city.

One of these markets lies not far from the Brooklyn Bridge, and has many stores, counters, and shops featuring the unusual foods that are used in Chinese cooking. This section is none other than the well-known "Chinatown" of the present day. Though the first Chinese immigrants came to this country as early as the first years after the Civil War in 1865, mostly as the farm and construction workers greatly needed at that time, their numbers were never great. Many more came with the flood of immigrants from every country in the world in the late 1800s, until the doors of immigration were practically closed to Asians and carefully controlled for almost every country that had immigrants to send. Others came in the wave just after World War II when more Chinese appeared on all our shores, and later, after 1948 when they could not come directly from China, made their way through Hong Kong and other countries of the East. Since that time, Chinese food has become popular with all people in the city and not something restricted only to the Chinese themselves—so much so that many non-Chinese visit Chinatown not only to enjoy its fine restaurants but also to market and cook for themselves in the Chinese manner.

Mott, Pell, and Doyers streets are the chief streets of the section, although many places spread out along East Broadway and Canal Streets. There you will find windows lined with pressed ducks, abalone—a favorite shellfish among the Chinese —mustard greens and lichee nuts. Many products imported from Hong Kong and Taiwan line the shelves: bamboo shoots, water chestnuts, oyster sauce, sesame oil, preserved ginger, thousand-year eggs, and many, many others. Tea houses have become more popular and are crowded in the afternoons with people who love the pastry shells and steamed buns that are served at "tea time" and which are filled mostly with pork or shrimp tid-bits. The pastry shops selling almond, walnut, and melon cookies are often standing open and inviting just next door. Gift shops are also a part of the Chinatown market scene, and there, small toys, trinkets, and souvenirs can be found, often costing very little. It is also possible to buy fine and expensive goods—articles and jewelry made of jade, and handsome furni-

A Chinese grocery window today
(below) and Chinese immigrants
on Mott Street in 1898 (opposite).
Chinese food has become popular
with all New Yorkers.

70

ture, mostly teakwood. If anything, the Chinatown "market town" keeps growing instead of shrinking, not so much because the number of Chinese immigrants has increased but because the interest in Chinese cooking and goods has spread.

In a matter of two or three blocks the market stands and store windows suddenly change. There are no longer the pressed ducks and lichee nuts, the Buddhas in windows, and the pagodas for telephone booths of the Chinatown streets. Instead, round and oval cheeses, large and small, hang from window poles and hooks, with unusual names like provolone, mozzarella, and beside them all sizes and shapes of sausages, salami, pepperoni, and other cold cuts not common to other markets or to other lunch tables. The windows and shelves are lined with tall heavy cans of olive oil, "Chianti" wine vinegars, all kinds of homemade pasta and noodles, pine nuts, jars of roast peppers, and eggplant appetizers. Beside these stands and store windows are the bakeries with long seeded breads in the windows, round and oval loaves, little white heaps of pizza dough, and special sesame cookies that are made there. These are Mulberry, Mott, and Grand streets of the Italian section—Little Italy it was once called—and further over, Market Street.

These Italian markets sell to people who live in the neighborhood, or to those who come from other sections for the

Cheeses hanging in a present-day Italian grocery (opposite) and an 1895 drawing of New York's "Little Italy."

73

quality of unusual food to be found there. Many are those who once lived in that crowded quarter but have moved to Staten Island or Queens and return every week—usually on Saturday, which has remained a favorite shopping day among the Italians —passing along the street to go from one small store to the other, faithful to the old butcher, the corner baker, the fish store, and the cheese man of the old days. Scattered throughout these streets are also small cafes or coffee shops, where they can stop and have an espresso, very strong coffee made in the European way, along with the many pastries and cakes that are sold there—rum cake, cheese cake, and all sorts of cream puffs and flaky-crust tarts filled with custard or cream. These shops also sell the famous Italian ices which come in so many styles and flavors, and the many-colored Italian ice creams that are not found in many places besides these few streets where "Little Italy" still manages to survive.

But the most famous markets of the Lower East Side were the Jewish markets. The thousands of immigrants from the ghettos of Eastern Europe poured into the tiny market stalls and set up their pushcarts on Hester Street, Orchard Street, Essex, Norfolk, and Ludlow. Because these streets became much like the Jewish quarters of old European cities, these were called the "Ghetto Market." The Jews in the Old World were used to living in a small community apart, both because they were forced to do so by the laws and ideas of Eastern European countries, and for their own protection and well-being. This way of living was largely followed in the New World, not only by the Jews who came here already used to such a small world or ghetto within the larger city, but by almost all newcomers, particularly if their language was not English.

These Jewish immigrants filled their "Ghetto Market" with the special foods they were used to. They stocked their push-carts and stalls with many kinds of smoked fish, lox, bagels, "kosher" chickens, kasha, sour cream, matzo meal, and black bread. There you would find also the chief dry-goods center of New York. For in their old Eastern European villages these immigrants had been used to the dry-goods vendor who went from house to house and from town to town with his "little bit of this and little bit of that." So, on the corner of Hester Street or Ludlow, this tradition, in different form, was preserved, and a vendor was still much like his Eastern European "cousin." For there he would stand with his pushcart or behind his stall, selling shoelaces and oilcloth, buttons and lace, ribbons and bolts of cloth. These vendors could be found there almost any time or day of the week, except that at sundown Friday until sundown Saturday, the streets and stalls would suddenly be empty and deserted. The Sabbath was strictly observed by the Jews who lived there, and this also had the effect of making Friday the busiest and most bustling "Market Day" of all. For then the women of the neighborhood would stock food and complete all cooking and other preparations for the Sabbath— the Friday evening meal always being a special one in the Jewish home. This led also to Sunday being a day when the markets of this area would reopen, and this made Sunday the important dry-goods market day just as Friday was the market day for food products. The Sunday dry goods markets were especially important, too, because other shops in the city were closed, and people from other neighborhoods would flock to shop there.

This custom has been preserved in the Orchard Street Market of the present day. The most important day of the Market is Sunday, and at that time hundreds of families press into the already crowded shops to buy the latest handbags and knit dresses, the most reasonable underwear and stockings. Dresses, coats, and umbrellas can be seen hanging from awnings, and tables stand on the sidewalk with other wares. Vendors sell pretzels, hot dogs, and knishes on street corners and for a moment it seems as though the clock has moved back seventy or eighty years, and only a few details have changed this from the old Hester Street market of other days.

But the very newest kind of market to be found all over New York was not part of New York life very many years ago. These are the Puerto Rican markets, now widespread in neighborhoods where large numbers of Puerto Rican families only recently have settled. There you will find the vegetables and fruits, the cuts of meat and special foods that these American-citizen "immigrants" were used to in San Juan and other Puerto Rican cities and villages. Some of them have become popular features of homes that are not Puerto Rican, but which have come to like the unusual tropical flavor of such favorites as mangos, coconuts, avocados, and plantains. A root vegetable like yucca which serves much as the potato does in many other diets has not gained much use outside of the Latin American

Religious articles are widely displayed in the Jewish . . .

. . . and Puerto Rican sections of the Lower East Side.

home. These foods you will find in Puerto Rican neighborhoods in many shapes, sizes, and kinds. Pork is the favorite meat product, and in addition to the usual pork cuts, pork rinds and such organs as pig's tongue, ear, and stomach appear in the "cuchifritos" or fried pork stands. Bacalao is the salt codfish which is deep-fried in the same manner. The highly spiced garlic sausage, "morcilla," is another common market sight.

All of these Puerto Rican favorites appear in the two main Puerto Rican neighborhoods that are part of the Lower East Side. These are the Delancey Street section and the Tompkins Square area. The Essex market, in which large numbers of Puerto Rican vendors are selling side by side with their Jewish and other market neighbors, is one of the largest. More and more Spanish signs appear each day, and "Latin" products like the ones already described. Spanish-speaking people stand behind the counters and crowd around each stand. But the Puerto Ricans of the neighborhood find not only food items there but also decorations for their homes. Many counters along the sides of the Essex Market show pictures and drawings of old San Juan, tiny statuettes of tropical birds, and many scarves and

77

handkerchiefs, fans and ashtrays display a colorful Puerto Rican theme. Many of these items are religious, and so figures of the Virgin Mary and other saints of the Roman Catholic Church will also be sold there along with rosary beads, prayer candles, and other religious articles for home use. In the Tompkins Square area there are whole altars set up in store fronts like the roadside altars found in many Latin countries.

In fact, the Tompkins Square area has become an important center for Puerto Rican families, although it is also the home of many Slavic groups—Polish and Ukrainian—and groups of young bearded boys and long-haired girls. Spreading out into nearby streets from East Tenth Street and Avenue A and Avenue B, the whole section is dotted with "bodegas" or small groceries that sell a variety of Puerto Rican goods. There you will find beans and rice, important foods in the Puerto Rican diet, sold "loose" from large burlap bags, just as different kinds of macaroni or pasta are sold in the old Italian market stores. All colors and flavors of "ices" are popular among the Puerto Rican children and adults just as they are in most Italian neighborhoods. Only these are called "piraguas" in the "Latin" sections, and the vendor is called a "piraguero." A refreshing drink, usually *not* found in other quarters of the city, is coconut juice, which in the summer becomes a great favorite.

Just as the Chinese, Italian, and Jewish markets and foods have become part of the mainstream eating habits of the whole city, so the Puerto Rican markets little by little have begun to serve neighborhoods and groups beyond their own island countrymen. No one would think a "knish" an odd food today in New York, or a "pizza" strange, although such food items were thought highly unusual fifty years ago—a part of the "strangers'" diet. In the same way, slowly, many foods from the Puerto Rican home are becoming more commonplace each day and less and less confined to neighborhoods and stores of the "Latin" newcomers' market of New York.

Ices called "piraguas" are a favorite of Puerto Ricans. Puerto Rican foods are becoming increasingly popular outside "Latin" neighborhoods, as Chinese, Jewish, and Italian foods did before them outside their neighborhoods.

79

A long time ago the sound of a street crier would cause doors to open, windows to be raised, and children and housewives to come running. Nowadays vendors are, for the most part, a fairly quiet lot. But often they rely on bells or chimes, or even music blaring from a record machine to attract their customers. This is particularly true of the ice-cream wagons and trucks that make the rounds of the neighborhoods. They have the same effect that a good street crier of the old days would always hope for: flocks of people all around him and at least a few sales among the crowd. Some of the ice-cream trucks even offer an "extra"—the promise of a ride to their young buyers, and for this purpose there is often a small merry-go-round at the side or in back of the truck, and circus music plays while children turn around and around on the backs of painted ponies. But most of the vendors, like the hot dog man under his umbrella stand, or the man selling chestnuts over hot coals, or the pretzel man with his warming-oven beside him, no longer roam the streets calling out their wares. They have a license to sell and usually a special spot to practice their trade. There they stand or sit waiting for shoppers to stop a moment for a snack or children to return from school. The day of the street crier is over. They expect their customers to come to *them*.

But once long ago the calls of the street crier were almost a special art. There were a surprising number and variety of them, and the talents of the street criers were remarked upon in many books and letters of the time. There still exists a handkerchief or scarf from 1814 that has many scenes of vendors with their cries painted and printed on it. CHOICE CLAMS, HERE'S YOUR ROCKAWAYS BEACH CLAMS, HERE'S YOUR FINE SAND CLAMS, was one favorite. PINE APPLES, FINE PINE APPLES was another. Or CAT TAILS, CAT TAILS, TO MAKE BEDS GOING was still another. In addition to the clam

Printed on cloth in 1814, this design shows City Hall surrounded by typical "Cries of New York."

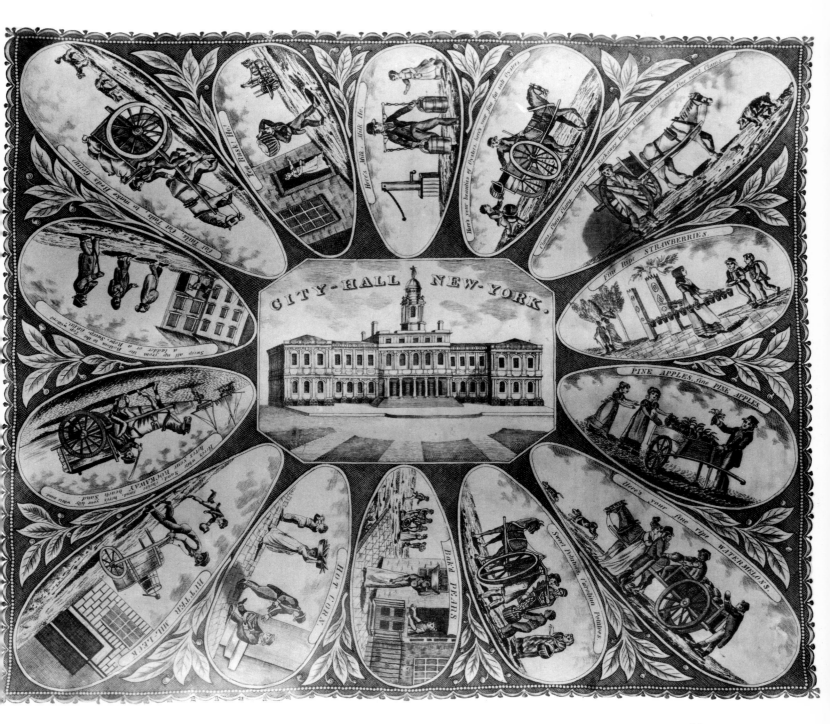

CITY-HALL NEW-YORK.

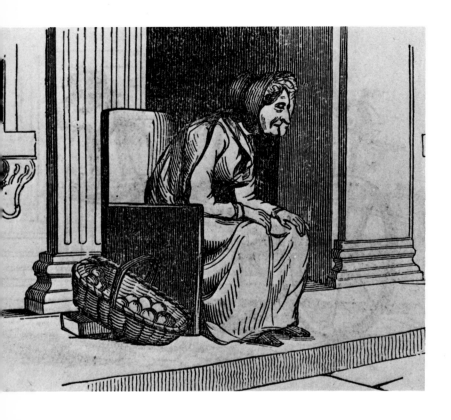

Some typical street vendors of old New York: the Old Apple Woman (above left), the Razor Strop man (above right), the Oyster Stand (below), and a soft drink peddler (opposite) photographed by Lewis W. Hine (George Eastman House Collection).

man, the pineapple man, and the cattail man, there was also the strawberry girl, the hot corn woman, the sweet potato man, the baked pear lady, the milk and butter man, the oyster boy, the tea man, the sand man, and many others. Up and down the streets they would go, calling their wares, knocking on doors, standing on street corners until they drew a crowd. Some of the vendors became such familiar sights they were known by special names according to where they stood or what they sold. On the corner of Bowery, Dover, Chatham, and Catherine streets stood the "Old Watch-House Wench selling Hot Corn," as the title of paintings and drawings of the time tell us. Later on, another vendor, so old and hunched she looked like a beggar, was made famous in another drawing: the Old Apple Woman at Stewart's. The book in which this engraving was printed told some of her story, for this woman sat for so many years in a special chair at the door of the same store that when the store moved into a new marble building, the owner, Mr. Stewart, had her chair moved to his new place of business.

In those days, many vendors came by in their wagons. Charcoal had so many uses in the home that the families impatiently waited for the charcoal wagon to come along. For the thirsty, a beer wagon would come by offering cold drinks to those who needed this kind of refreshment on their travels or at work in the middle of the day. Among the most popular callers were those who sharpened the household tools and the kitchen scissors and knives. The "razor-strop man" was a special favorite of the men, and many parents and grandparents in our homes today remember when the "scissors grinder" would make the rounds of neighborhoods not so very long ago. The iceman and the milkman are easily remembered by many more and are sometimes still found practicing an old trade.

But what is sold on street corners has varied according to the neighborhood and the habits of the customers they serve. With each new wave of immigrants a new kind of street vendor is added to the long list of the past. In addition to the hot dogs, pretzels, and ice cream that remain the most common items sold by vendors on the streets, there are now Italian and Puerto Rican ices, knishes, egg rolls, and the bacalaos and pastels that are favorites of the Puerto Rican community.

Many of the vendors have small stands or wagons or else they have counters in a storefront that opens out onto the street. Pickle stands are very popular along Broome Street, and pizza stands are common everywhere in New York. Sausage and pepper places have sprung up and are especially concentrated around Mott and Mulberry Streets. Cuchifrito stands serving a variety of fried pork things are to be found in many largely Puerto Rican neighborhoods, but are especially frequent on the Lower East Side in both the Tompkins Square area and around Clinton and Delancey streets—in the old section where the de Lancey mansion once used to stand so long ago, and where street criers themselves were rarely encountered but could be heard in the busy streets nearby.

Vendors are still common on the streets of the Lower East Side.

84

Townhouses

and Townspeople

Most of all a neighborhood is the people who live inside its boundaries and streets—who they are, where they live, and how they live. A neighborhood reflects much about the people who live there, and the people who live there do much to form and change a place. But a neighborhood reflects, too, what people cannot control about where and how they live. This has much to do with jobs and money, the training and education of people, and their numbers. Cities and the neighborhoods within them act upon each other. Sometimes in sharing problems and working to solve them, cities and neighborhoods, and the people who live there, do not see things the same way. Sometimes one or another of them do not choose the best ways to meet changes and to guide them. Then a neighborhood declines. It becomes run-down and ugly. People are not proud to live there. Their lives become unhappy, either because they move out when, had things been only a little better, they might have wished to stay. Or else they must stay because there seems no way out, even when they want it. There is nothing sadder than when a town has failed its townhouses and townspeople or when *they* have begun to fail the town.

But often people and towns fight to keep their neighborhoods alive and well. This has happened throughout the history of the city, and it will always happen. Just as neighborhoods have become run down, so, often they will rise up. The story of a neighborhood is also the story of its *ups* and *downs*. It is not only told by "hidden houses" and "burned timbers" which must be specially dug up and found. It is also a story easy to read with one's own eyes in the daylight of everyday. A walk along a city block will show it. There, side by side, will stand rows and rows of houses, each one much like the next—even sometimes a twin. Yet one will face the street faded and old,

A Lower East Side tenement in 1920 (above) and neighborhood tenements today (opposite).

92

broken down and ruined. Beside it, another will look out with new paint and mended housefront, some sign that makes it fresh and bright among its neighbors, as though it lives today as well as yesterday, no matter what its age and style. The story of a neighborhood is that story, too—the house after house and the street after street that make it up. For the story of a neighborhood is most of all the townhouses and townspeople we will find there and who still speak to us today without a word.

Some of the houses from the 1700s and 1800s can still be found on New York streets. Most of them are clustered in the downtown area, and are most numerous in some of the blocks of the Lower East Side. While almost all of the oldest houses in Greenwich Village have been carefully restored and saved, those of the Lower East Side are often neglected, ignored, and left to be torn down and ruined. When they are singled out for attention, spruced up and cared for, these same homes rank with the best examples of old houses in the nation.

What are such houses like, or what *were* they like when they "lived" back in their own time? They were in the English style, but always a little behind what was in fashion in England at that time. This was because the settlers were copying and remembering what they had left behind in their old towns and villages, and they often hired city planners and builders who had already won fame in the old country for earlier designs. The Dutch houses had already begun to disappear from New York life throughout the 1700s, and the Great Fire of 1835 took a final toll so that they vanished completely from New York streets. It was no wonder the Dutch houses always went up like torches, for they were made of wood and the oldest ones had thatched roofs that easily broke into flame. In the early settle-

The Great Fire of 1835 destroyed the last of the original Dutch houses in New York. This scene depicts colonial fire-fighting around 1750.

93

ment of New Amsterdam there were no matches, and fires were left to burn all night. Sometimes such low smoldering fires broke loose to become raging fires. Stories were common that in running to the home of a neighbor to get burning embers, the returning housewife sent sparks flying in the wind, and many a barn and house of New Amsterdam was lost that way.

The English townhouses that lined the streets in 1700 and 1800 were of many kinds, many styles, and reflected many small changes over a long period. They were row homes made of brick. By the middle and end of the 1800s brick was no longer the fashion and in its place brownstone became the favorite material for building.

But the early New York house built in the English style was popular a long time. It was originally called the Colonial or Georgian style, which described one and the same thing— "Georgian" simply meant the style under the Georges of England, during the days of the English colonies, and "Colonial," of course, referred to the same period of time. When the colonies were no longer under English rule but had gained their freedom to become the United States of America, this style came to be called Federal. These houses—whichever of the three names is used—were three, three and one half, or four stories high, and made of brick that ranged from yellow pink in color to a deep red.

When such houses remain standing, their dates can roughly be known by the kind, color, and placement of bricks. Another common clue is how the bricks are joined together, and what material it is that joins them. For example, mortar made with cement was not used until after 1850, and so this is one easy way to know if a house dates from before 1850 or after. The earlier ones used a mortar made of a mixture of lime and sand, and so instead of having the later uniform color of cement, it took on the special color of the sand, which varied

English row houses, like these on Henry Street, bring the past into the present, and must be preserved for the future.

94

from place to place and from time to time. But besides the materials themselves, the most obvious ways we can date a house is by the style of its doorways and windows, and the type of cornice found there—a cornice being the overhanging where house joins roof. These cornices were plaster in early days, but were usually made of wood after 1750. They were more decorated in some periods and more delicate in others, and this became another way to determine the general date a house was built. Doorways kept changing from one period to another, going from a plain style around 1700 to a formal bracket above the door and other differences after that. Windows show even greater changes, for about 1700 they had very small panes of glass, and often a brick arch above the window, and at that time only the bottom part of the window was moveable. Later on, the window panes became much larger and airier, and wood frames replaced the brick around the window. Also in this later period shutters were added, though even the shutters themselves became a way to know how early or how late a house was built. For even they were different in size, in decoration, in number of panels, and in how they were hung. Even the hardware of any sort on a house tells a great deal about its age. Knobs and locks on these houses were always much lower than they would be on a modern door, and the fastenings on the shutter and cellar doors looked and worked differently from the present day.

What is most interesting about these houses is that we may not only read about them in books but may see them standing on our streets to tell their tale. Those that are prized and well kept all in a row have become some of the most valuable houses in the city. Those in Greenwich Village, where whole streets have been restored, are good examples. In the Lower East Side, though there are some like the few on Henry Street, rarely are whole blocks cared for and intact. The Schermerhorn Row project of the riverfront renewal will be a welcome remedy for this great loss and lack. Other old houses can be found on many streets not far from the entrance to Brooklyn Bridge, where they have been spared while their neighbors were taken, and in the Corlear's Hook area a few blocks from the river. Though the city, state, and national governments have taken some interest in restoring these old houses in old "towns," sometimes the overload of all the city problems causes it to tear down these sections—sometimes because they must, and sometimes because they have not thought through all the ways a city must meet its people's needs. While traffic expansion and improvements have usually cost the most in lives of houses —even more than the building of vast apartment developments—many cities plan new expressways, tunnel, and bridge approaches in other ways. Many go underground, or some go around the city, or if this is impossible, take routes less damaging to the old town. There are many sides to such a story and decisions are often made after much consideration and long delay. Most of all, such changes require more and deeper *overall* planning that goes further than merely today or the next few years. It must take into account the history of the city as a whole—past, present, and future—what the city is and what it wants to be.

What were some of the famous landmarks to meet a sorry fate? First, it must be said that sometimes houses pass through many lives before traffic changes and new buildings sweep them away. Some may end up still standing, but only wrecks of their former selves. Others are restored to their old elegance and charm. And the third way is for them to disappear and be replaced by completely different things that include no sign of the former life of the place.

One house that went through many lives in its place near the approach to Brooklyn Bridge before it became one of the many tolls that new construction took, was the famous Walton House built in 1752. Its proud owner, William Walton, had

The Walton House of 1752. Such houses may have many lives before they fall victim to new construction.

turned it into the most fashionable house in New York before the Revolutionary War in 1776. He entertained there on such a scale and in such elegance and taste that the British used it as an example of the wealth of the colonists whom they felt should be more heavily taxed. This house was at 326–28 Pearl Street, and the social life of the city was often said to center in that area. After the Revolutionary War, the house became the first Bank of New York, and so the business life of the new nation had an elegant home there. When the Bank of New York moved farther uptown—as so much of New York life did in the next half century after that—the famous Walton House knew less elegant and always harder and harder times, for it was already a boardinghouse around 1800, and described by one reporter as representing American taste and elegance "a little worse for wear."

But what of a whole building that *does* remain in good condition? How does it stay handsome and intact from those old days? The answer is that most of the time it is never permitted to get very far along the road to decay and ruin. It is cared for almost every step along the way—perhaps more or less so at different times—but over its one hundred and fifty or more years, it is kept up, retouched, and shown attention. This is clearly shown in some details of houses that are today in almost as good repair as in their newest and finest days. These become finds and treasures of the present day, worth seeking out, and worth a look and study. One such detail is the doorway of St. Patrick's School in the Italian section, at Mott and Prince streets, not too far away from the Italian markets that are much better known landmarks of the neighborhood.

Children run up and down the pavement and steps of this old school, and in and out of classrooms, as though theirs were like any other school in the city and not one of the oldest Federal buildings in New York. They wave at strangers from windows and doors without showing any sign that they learn their lessons in rooms used by other children so long ago.

In 1825 when this building was built, it was an orphans' home and part of old St. Patrick's Church that stood beside it. St. Patrick's moved uptown to its famous and handsome home on Fifth Avenue and Fiftieth Street when it became not just a neighborhood church but a grand cathedral. But the orphans' home stayed behind on Prince and Mott streets, and slowly was changed to a general school. As a neighborhood school of the old St. Patrick's parish, it is treated as any other building in those crowded blocks. Only by looking closely at it does it become more than an old building—a new reminder of that still graceful and handsome Federal style that otherwise would have died out in that old place. The almost one hundred and fifty years of wear and tear, of "ups and downs" have given it if anything a deeper character and a dignity all its own. Its

99

doorway stands with quiet pride on an otherwise common and modern street, showing off its fine wood panels, the slender columns that support it on either side, the beautiful fanlight window that calls attention to its role in another time, the graceful keystone arch that curves around the door in striking white. This doorway having survived, endured, offers a strong and pleasant contrast to life that hurries on around, beyond it. It has become more precious in *ours* than it was in its *own* time.

Unfortunately, a mark of elegance from a still later time was ground into the dust and has not lived to tell its tale. Yet nothing was a standard of greater beauty, elegance, wealth, and taste than the beautiful hotels that lined downtown Broadway around 1850. They made Broadway the most fashionable part of New York with an elegance surpassing even the Fifth Avenue and Park Avenue of our present day. One of the most fashionable of these was the St. Nicholas Hotel on Broadway

The doorway of St. Patrick's School (opposite) remains a living treasure of the past in our time, but the elegant St. Nicholas Hotel (above) is gone and can only be read about in books.

between Broome and Spring streets, in the general area of the approaches to the Holland Tunnel today. The fine white marble front of this hotel was widely hailed and spoken of in its own day—almost a landmark to visitors who came to the city—and the most famous place to pass by and promenade, on foot or in the handsome carriages that drove by. It was called a "white palace" in many writings that describe it, and its other marble furnishings, its velvet, silk, and satin trappings inside, were said to be a grand and breathtaking sight. It and its handsome neighbors—"white palace" or not—all came down one day. It is only one of the former landmarks of New York that now can only be read about in books.

But new structures have gone up in other sections of the Lower East Side, always trying to deal with the changes and increasing numbers that have flocked and concentrated in this always overflowing downtown New York. They are taller for the most part and house as many as six hundred families at a time. Perhaps a few of the sturdiest, the best kept, and the finest models will one day remain in future times to mark the record of our present day. Any that survive will take their place in a wider "time" that includes many centuries and many styles, in which we also would, hopefully, want our own place and our own part.

But what are the buildings and houses that make up *our* contribution? Along with the large apartment buildings that have been part of the city's life for at least eighty or ninety years, there have been more and more examples of a more recent form of housing—the cooperatives and projects that dot the Lower East Side area. These sometimes are built on such a large scale that they become whole neighborhoods themselves.

Large projects like the Lower East Side's Vladeck Houses may become neighborhoods within neighborhoods.

To understand why this is so, you have only to see some of the old and not so old slums of the city that they have—always with high hopes—replaced.

These hot, crowded, dark, decaying places—called slums or tenements or ghettos in our modern day—have been part of city life for over a hundred years. But they became a more difficult problem as the population swelled after the great periods of immigration and growth all over the world. In the years when these problems became so serious—around 1880 and thereabouts—people in other countries were sorely needed to help the country expand, grow, and develop its riches. With no more than a promise of a job, people flocked to the country's shores; and though their work and labor were required, little provision was made for these vast new numbers, their special problems and, most of all, the fact that they were homeless, poor, and were making a new life in a strange place that granted them little living space and room. Also, something similar occurred during and after World War II—from 1941 on —when large numbers of Blacks left their homes in the South for new jobs and new lives in the North, they, too, finding a city ill-prepared to cope with such numbers and such change.

When these "old" slums and "new" ones reach a point when they become so crowded, so run-down, so unpleasant, and even dangerous in the city's midst, new planning and new effort is made to solve the problems they present. To do this, the city, state, and national governments have banded together to act in behalf of troubled citizens, hopeful that these improvements will be more lasting than others of the past.

Often slum conditions are so bad because so many people share a living space intended for far fewer, yet these families have not enough money to pay for the additional room they really need. Rents in the city are sometimes controlled, but many times there is not a good balance between the number of low, or even average, cost apartments and the number of

This community faucet in a tenement hall was photographed by Lewis W. Hine in 1910. Such slums have been a part of city life for more than a century. (George Eastman House Collection)

people who want them. So, among many others, two ways have become more widespread and common in the Lower East Side, for the city, the state, and the national governments to join forces to meet this problem. One way has been for them to pay the cost of building large modern buildings and developments which the tenants can then pay back by "buying" their apartments, placing a down-payment on them and then paying low maintenance charges along the way—one of the many kinds of "cooperatives" that exist. Another has been to meet the cost of such needed building completely through loans and taxes, and charging the new tenants less per room than in other buildings, in this way permitting them to have more space to meet their needs in the crowded city of today. Many large projects have come into being as a result of this practice.

Sometimes such cooperatives and projects have built into them many neighborhood improvements and features only the city can provide. This includes playgrounds and parks, community centers, and neighborhood houses. One example of these improved recreation areas can be found in the Jacob Riis Houses, not very far from the East River, and not very far from the Tenth Street section around Tompkins Park. This playground is the result of a long study of shapes and forms, games and recreation all over the world, with the result that experts and students from other countries now visit it to get new and modern ideas that have been already realized in this park. The playground is full of treehouses and nests of rocks, of hanging trellises and swirls of hanging objects, of sliding areas, and running and climbing hills. In wood, stone, and concrete, in springy foam rubber and sturdy plastic, imaginative shapes and safe "fall" areas have been built, so that children of all ages spring and leap across the park. There, away from the city streets, they safely and more happily play in the well-planned and well-designed surroundings that have taken them and their play into account. Next to the playground is a huge amphi-

Projects like the Jacob Riis Houses with their imaginative playground are one answer to urban slum problems.

106

theater where plays, concerts, special programs and shows can be performed and enjoyed by all in the neighborhood. Night lights make it possible for this to be a pleasant way to spend an evening in the heat of the city.

The "future" city of New York will most likely more and more resemble this one—huge buildings with large recreational areas built in, and some stores and many necessary services also found in their midst. Thus, these have become almost "neighborhoods within neighborhoods" all by themselves, and in so doing they have joined the many "towns within a town" of the Lower East Side that already and for so long have had a place there.

The future of New York may lie in giant apartment complexes with recreation areas and other facilities built in.

*A*nd what of the townspeople of the Lower East Side? While their townhouses have undergone such change, and their streets, and their sidewalks, how have *they* changed?

Though it is easy to think that in old Dutch days people looked alike and spoke the same language, this is very far from true. It has been recorded that in 1643 eighteen different languages were spoken in the old town. Although—besides English—Hebrew, Yiddish, Spanish, Italian, Chinese, and several Slavic languages are spoken in the Lower East Side streets of the present day, there is no reason to believe the number of languages would go beyond that early figure already reached in New Amsterdam's first days. Also, there were people of many races living together in that past time. For in addition to the white Europeans of the town, the Indians, who had lived there long before them, were everywhere to be seen. In time of peace, they came and went freely, taking part in Market Day and celebrations, working and living in and near the boundaries of the town. War upset this way of life, although when peace was won again, people returned to the former good relations that existed, until once more war drove settler and Indian far apart. Blacks were also very commonly to be seen in the settlement's first days, though often in early times as slaves, or sometimes as "half-slaves," which meant they could work off their term of service to freedom. But quite early there were freed slaves who were much more common than one might think—so much so that there was a quarter of the city where freed slaves made up all the inhabitants, the whole area which is now Chatham Square and where Chinatown is located and has grown.

But most of all it was the numbers of people that were so different. There were 500 people who lived in all New Amsterdam in 1645, and 1,500 made it a thriving and prosperous town in 1665. By 1830, after the colony had won its freedom, it was already growing crowded with its 200,000 population and expansion still on its way. Today when more than that number live on the Lower East Side all by itself, and the whole city is already at 9,000,000 and pressing on beyond, such figures seem almost amusing and more than a little quaint. Of the more than 300,000 to which the Lower East Side neighborhood has grown, the Jewish, Italian, Puerto Rican, and Black groups make up the highest percentages of people who remain there.

But aside from numbers, languages, color, race, and such ways of considering groups and not the individuals of which they are all made, how have the people changed? Their work has shifted from tiny farms, and trade with the trading company that made their laws and very much ran their lives, to the millions of jobs, each different from the next, in factories, offices, at counters, trucks, on land and sea and air. Each life— in the old town and the new—can be seen as difficult and pleasurable in its own way. Townspeople of the past had much hard work and a hard life in wresting from the wilderness a town. Yet they also had room and space to live in, good air, fresh water, more inner peace and calm than in our day.

With their free time, what did they do? The men in old Dutch days liked nothing better than sitting outdoors or in taverns smoking their pipes and drinking their beer, talking to neighbors of past days, new problems, and swapping jokes, stories, and tales. Even the women found recreation in their talk, taking the same path to the town wall, where, a little ways beyond, a fresh stream flowed. There they did their wash, drying their linens on large rocks, and gossiping with the other townswomen whom they met. The young girls, talking and laughing as they went, walked this way with large bundles of clothes, while young men of the town waited for them to pass. This meeting place became so common, it was called the Maiden's Lane. Simple enjoyments of this kind, and the Market Day and holiday celebrations that they loved, were almost the only recreation the busy Dutch townspeople could find time for. Nowadays while people work hard and long hours at their jobs, they have, nonetheless, a good portion of free time and eagerly turn to recreations of all kinds.

But all New York townspeople of every time and of different ways have loved and flocked to all manner and types of parades. Today they are more elaborate than in past times—ticker tape flooding the streets, huge floats passing reviewing stands, parade queens, flowers, bands, majorettes, animals, and thousands of spectators lining the streets and overflowing the sidewalks. In older days a simple band was all that would be required to draw large crowds. Soldiers would march with them and curious bunches of people would gather on the spot, and that would already be considered an event and a parade. In immigrant days, bands were also used in another way, for many immigrants were used to music in their old villages and towns—the German immigrants especially loved music of every character and kind. They formed little bands mainly to play for their own amusement, or in parks, on sidewalks and street corners, not to speak of in the taverns and little coffee

G. Brown N.A.
1879

112

A German street band of 1879 (opposite). Today, bongo players are often heard in the parks and playgrounds of the Lower East Side (right).

houses of the time. Bands have remained a common source of recreation and amusement even in our day—not only military bands and the parade bands of adults, but drum and bugle corps that draw so many teenagers who play instruments to their ranks, along with drum majors and majorettes who flock there for the color and excitement of parades. But increasingly more popular each day are the "steel bands," made of specially tuned drums, that draw many Black and Puerto Rican boys because of their West Indian flavor and beat. Many people also throng around bongo drum players in parks, playgrounds, and on the city streets, or surround the many guitar players who

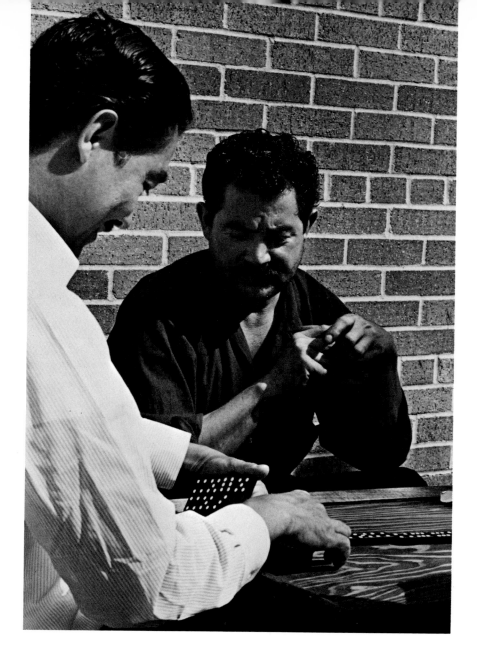

Dominoes is a favorite game of Puerto Ricans.

often turn up in gatherings to play one of the most popular instruments of our day.

A walk through Tompkins Square will turn up many small gatherings of this type, and while the young are mostly involved in their own activity and in their own little section of the park, across from them, off in another corner, the older men in all neighborhoods and "towns" find amusement of another kind. In their small groups, Ukrainian men love most to play at cards, almost silently or else they exchange whole conversations and remarks in their own tongue, mixing in English words that stand out strangely in context. Meanwhile, off in another corner, the Puerto Rican men play the dominoes they prefer to almost any other game. And still other small groups stand watching games of checkers or, much rarer, chess. And while there is no such area in Tompkins Park, not far off near Houston Street or farther away in the Mulberry Street section of New York, Italian men are gathered together for a more active sport—"bocce," with the balls and alleys the game requires, and the concentration, the tense scenes of measuring spaces between balls, the debate and argument it inspires, until finally it is too dark to see.

Equipment in playgrounds is enough to entertain the very young—slides, swings, sandboxes. Others of all ages seek entertainment indoors, in front of television sets, in movie houses. Older boys and girls, besides gathering around bongo players or the folk singers with guitars, play their transistor radios in the streets, dancing in playgrounds, and sending the sound of their favorite records and "combos" blaring into the streets. For those who are more actively inclined, basketball nets are everywhere to be seen, and games of handball and baseball are often played in roped off, closed-to-traffic streets, or in the school playgrounds that are always crowded with one kind of recreational activity or another. Sometimes two or three boys prefer pitching pennies to any other sport, and still popular is the form of baseball that is conveniently played against the walls. Hopscotch or pozzi games are sometimes played on the sidewalks or in the street, though nowadays it is unnecessary to draw the giant squares with chalk, for many playgrounds have the outlines already drawn and waiting for players to put them to use.

But some of the most unusual entertainment "comes to town"—brought there by groups which draw large audiences of

Whereas hurdy-gurdies were once heard in the Lower East Side (below), long-haired guitar players often provide the street music today (opposite).

both children and adults, and particularly on summer evenings when there seems more time and interest in special activities of every kind. East River Park offers people from the neighborhood band, orchestra, and jazz concerts, and now and then a program is given on the South Street docks. Touring actors offer plays by Shakespeare, light comedies and musicals, puppet and marionette shows in parks and playgrounds, some with amphitheaters, some with a simple put-together stage.

Sometimes even more unusual programs come into neighborhoods from far places. Such an event was the Children's Theater of Hong Kong, which included Chinatown in its world tour. Children and adults flocked to watch this famous theater of children—all from eight to seventeen years of age—who learn their art in the well-known Spring and Autumn Theatrical Chinese School in Hong Kong. There they acted out the classical Chinese plays with the clanging music which is performed right on the stage. The children, all dressed in brilliant costumes, moved gravely or delicately, waving fly whisks, doing somersaults, acting and dancing the ancient tale of the White Snake Lady in Combat. Chinatown is rich in other special entertainments—one of the most popular being the Lion Dance performed by the men and boys to celebrate the coming of the Chinese New Year. To the clanging and whirring music that is played in the open street, the dancers, in colorful costumes topped by a great lion's head and mane, weave in and out along Pell and Mott streets to usher in the year.

In the same way, the Italian section celebrates its own special moments and events. This takes the form of elaborate festivals, often over several days or a whole week, to celebrate a saint's day. There, long block parties take place in streets that are closed off to traffic for the occasion. Electric light bulbs are strung across the streets and turn them into a giant carnival that goes on and on into the night. Special stands are set up everywhere to sell the deep-fried pastry, the sausage sand-

Chinatown is especially rich in festivals and entertainments.

119

wiches, the raw clams, the eggplant dishes, pizza, and lasagna that keep people crowding around counters, eating off napkins and paper plates, and passing money over other people's out-stretched arms and heads. Other stands are full of bowling pins, balloons, and plates to be knocked down or popped, or else there are spinning wheels that stop at lucky or unlucky num-bers, as the case may turn out to be. People walk hand in hand, pressed against the always thickening crowds, and go off eating their ices and pastries into the night.

In Puerto Rican neighborhoods there are sometimes, though not often, candlelight processions on religious holidays and in honor of the most popular church patrons or saints. People of the neighborhood and from the church wind their long procession through nearby streets with lighted candles, singing, and carrying the church statues and holy objects as they go.

Meanwhile, in settlement houses and community centers where so much recreational activity is concentrated in these days, there are more and more events that highlight African culture, which is still unfamiliar though of much interest, to both the Black and non-Black population of New York. Guests, in some instances, have been invited to speak, appearing in their traditional African robes and headdress as they tell about the African nations from which they come. Films are shown of African dances and tribal costumes, and in the workshops of these centers more and more African masks and carvings are made, especially by Black children who are proud of and attracted by the distant cultures that centuries back had been their own.

In early New York days, as in most towns and villages no matter where they are in all the world, one of the most popular entertainments was the circus. And when circus time was no-where near, people flocked to see the strange wild animals at the zoo. One of the best-known zoos was, for a long time, found

Barnum's American Museum was a popular attraction in mid-nineteenth century New York, along with zoos, circuses, and lotteries.

not in far off Central Park or in the distant Bronx, but for the Downtown of that day, close by—on the Bowery near Bayard Street. The Zoological Institute, or the "Bowery Menagerie" as it was sometimes called, presented tigers and elephants, monkeys and lions to the people who flocked there and who were excited by tales of wild animals loose and keepers in danger—sometimes a fact of real life and sometimes imagined.

Another early "entertainment" was the lottery drawing which was usually a gala event on downtown Broadway, held before a wide public of ticket holders and guests who came for the excitement and suspense. These lottery drawings went all the way back to the earliest Dutch days, for it has been recorded that in 1655 the Dutch raised money through the lottery to pay for poor relief. Later in 1746, under English rule, lotteries were run to pay for defense and fortification of the town. Now and then lotteries were run to raise funds for schools, and one famous one had all its proceeds go to start King's College, later Columbia University. Though lotteries became illegal in the middle of 1800, they continued to interest New Yorkers who wanted them to be part of the state's ways and life. Recently another New York State lottery came into being, and is still held in the present day, with the money earmarked for education as it had been in many cases long ago.

But whether the entertainments, recreations, or diversions are old or new, whether they take place indoors or out, whether they are organized or come about by chance, whether they have been part of towns no longer existent or present ones, rapidly changing as they are, they still help us to see best of all how people live or lived. Through them, we know much more of what a town was or is, and how a neighborhood is becoming. These enjoyments of free time have gradually moved from the kitchen fire and the path to the town stream where they were still closely linked with work, with errands, and with chores, to the entertainment strictly for and in itself—at the movies, before the TV set, in parks, playgrounds, amphitheaters, and halls. Even the most easy-to-have entertainment of them all, talking, tells us something about our towns and neighborhoods and change. For this too, has moved to a new location—the old talking over fences is replaced by the street corner, the door-step, the fire escape, and the rooftop chatting and gathering of our day.

The people, the houses, and the ways of a past time have left an imprint on each city neighborhood we might pass. The present is leaving its traces as it moves. It goes backward and forward, catching up old things almost ready to be lost yet worth preserving, and scooping out fresh places for future things not yet completed. So, old clipper ships are reappearing in the harbor, and "steel bands" spring up where no need was ever felt for them before. One house is rediscovered, touched up, restored—workmen, painters hovering over it, attentive to its needs—while right next door wreckers swing the giant wrecking ball to send walls down and to make way for new structures in their midst. All over the city tin patches gleam in windows that have been knocked out—the telltale sign that these buildings, too, are marked for wrecking, being made ready, as though to say: Beware, something will happen, some-thing will change. Streets will be widened, or "vest-pocket" parks will be built, new arms of highways will meet there, or cut-offs and exits to expressways will be added.

But, just now, old restored houses, broken-down tenements, new projects, and huge cooperative developments are still living side by side, though approaches to bridges, entrances to tun-nels, new expressways have taken more of them each day. They

have forced neighborhoods to *give*, and this has usually meant *giving up* something already there. While this is always necessary for growing and for change, it raises many questions. What must be given up? How will it be decided? Will the right things go, and the best remain? Or does the giant wrecking ball decide too many times before men think and choose?

We have seen both wise decisions and glaring mistakes made in lives of cities. Right now an important instance of this kind faces every neighborhood and every city in some way. In the Lower East Side, the planning of the Lower Manhattan Expressway, which has been in progress for some years, means something will have to give, give way to change. And sometime in the future, even whatever will stand there in that place must itself face new upheaval—for there will be another future after that.

In the case of the Lower Manhattan Expressway, the result—new avenues for traffic and space to build them—is sorely needed. But hard questions still remain, not only for this project, but for countless others. What is it that will go? Can such a superhighway be built underground, overhead, in some new, not-yet-known way, that would take cars and trucks off city streets and still leave old houses and old neighborhoods intact and mostly standing? Should what the city must *give up* be its rows upon rows of old brick and brownstone houses, its small shops, its old markets, its sense of neighborhood itself? They have already survived fire and war as well as the erosion caused by nature and man. Now they face the giant ball swinging and swaying in their path. Can the city afford to lose with each new project more and more of its old roots and still have much to do with the city it once was? Or will its giant swinging ball devour it bit by bit, destroying the city's very *self*? Does the city, in fact, know what it wants to be—which means do the people know? How much is the future built on layer after layer of past and present, and how much is it built on fresh ideas and not-

How do we decide what must go in a city? Will the right things go and the best remain? City planners are faced with many such difficult questions.

125

yet-dreamed-of ways? How much should be preserved of what has already been and how much should be a new start, a new direction? Do words like old and new mean anything if something *old* is fresh and something *new* already on the road to ruin and decay? Must neighborhoods themselves *go* to make way for future things, or should something about them be preserved? Do they stand for more than the eye can *see*? Must the expressways, the industrial plants, and the apartment complexes that we so sorely need, go through the very oldest sections of our towns, or can they go somehow *around, under, over,* and *beyond* them? Do costs make this impossible, and, if so, are there other ways we haven't thought of to face and meet such costs? Does the swinging giant ball cost more in *lives* than *money,* deciding how it is that people who clear out will live?

These are some of the city's questions—if cities could talk and people would listen. These are the questions to which answers, advice, and arguments are given every day—by experts in each field, by commissioners, by mayors, and by thousands of people who go to public hearings and who vote. All these things—planning, discussions, public hearings, elections, awarding of contracts, building—are stages along the way. And they take several years. Yet this is what the present is most of all about—deciding future and past things, as well as going on. The present is the friction they produce—the past still wanting so very much to be, and the future impatient to become. The present is how they come together, and also how they draw apart. The present is the city contracting, expanding, giving, taking—the way it moves and breathes. For the present is time *alive* instead of *still.* It is not *still* as past things like New Amsterdam are *still,* or, as future things, like those on drawing boards, in sketches, must be still. The present is this very moment when the city lives—what it has saved and what it is becoming, all shifting, turning, changing and breathing in the day and night of its own time and place.

Bibliography

Feininger, Andreas and Lyman, Susan E. *The Face of New York.*

Hults, Dorothy Niebrugge. *New Amsterdam Days and Ways.*

Huxtable, Ada Louise. *Classic New York.*

Kouwenhoven, John. *The Columbia Historical Portrait of New York.*

Lockwood, Sarah M. *New York, Not So Little and Not So Old.*

Lyman, Susan E. *The Story of New York.*

Nicholson, Arnold (illustrations by Penelope Hartshorne). *Notes on the Design and Architectural Detail of Philadelphia Row Houses, 1740–1850.*

Saunders, Wendreth. *Building Brooklyn Bridge.*

Schoener, Allon. *Portal to America: The Lower East Side, 1870–1925.*

Senior, Clarence. *Strangers Then Neighbors.*

Silver, Nathan. *Lost New York.*

Veglahn, Nancy. *The Spider of Brooklyn Heights.*

Index